Never Alone

A Chronicle

by
Paul Gerhard Tittel

May 2015

Published by CPS Communication Production Services, Inc., Parkton, MD
Printed by H&N Printing & Graphics, Timonium, MD

ISBN 978-0-692-28262-5

Table of Contents

Forward

The writings on these pages of the "Never Alone" story are strictly from memory and memories without any notes or a diary of the events that go back for seventy years for the war stories and sixty years with me taking that bold step of escaping as a sixteen year old from that total eristic regime the East German Communists. These events made a photographic imprint on me, and, therefore, they were by no means easy to forget. I am certain that there must have been incidents similar to mine, these people were either shot to death or could not get their story together. The Berlin Wall was known to many, and how many lives were taken there was also recorded. But the long border running from the north at the Baltic Sea, to the south at the Bavarian border, had many more fatalities than has been recorded and there seems never to have been an interest to make that public. The incident of the two men in their twenties being too close to the border and being shot to death one week before my escape, and in the same area, makes my point.

This story, "Never Alone," has been written because, over a time of roughly fifty-eight years living in my new home, the United States, many curious people I have met – friends, strangers, associates, neighbors, people from all walks of life – have asked me how I made it, from over there to over here, and one episode led to the next. "Never Alone" has many more stories to it, but memory with time and age is fading swiftly. I have also known many people who wanted to write their interesting life stories (memoirs), and they never did and I, like them, almost did not either, but these curious people made me finally put my story on paper and to them I bow in gratitude with sincere thanks. In his latest publication "Nearing Home," Billy Graham points to how difficult it is for older people to use the pen and put something constructive on paper. I can certainly concur with Billy Graham about what old age has to offer. We know, without the strength God gives us every day, we could accomplish nothing. It is by His divine guidance that we are sustained day by day.

Acknowledgments

Throughout my life's journey I can say, that I never felt alone; I had someone constantly watching over me, at my side, guiding me, protecting me, helping me, giving me sound advice: this coming from no one other than my heavenly maker. It is therefore with gratitude, and it is more than proper, to dedicate these few words to Him who made everything in my life possible. I thought it would be mostly fitting to use the beautiful words of Dr. Martin Luther's explanation of the Apostle's Creed's first article where it says:

> *I believe that God has made me and all creatures; that He has given me my body and soul, eyes, ears and all my members, my reason and all my senses and still preserves them; also clothing and shoes, meat and drink, house and home, wife and children, fields, cattle, and all my goods; that He richly and daily provides me with all that I need to support this body and life; that He defends me against all danger and guards and protects me from all evil, and all this purely out of fatherly divine goodness and mercy, without any merit or worthiness in me; for all which it is my duty to thank and praise, to serve and obey Him. This is most certainly true.*

Furthermore, this book is dedicated to my oldest sister, Elisabeth, who took on motherhood at age eighteen under extremely difficult circumstances (after my mother died at age 44); she managed to raise her three younger siblings with love and dedication. My gratitude also goes to Suzanne Lieske and Nancy Wachter who helped me to prepare this manuscript.

Chapter 1
Our Family Life in a Real Wartime Situation

I was born as the sixth child of my family on April 3, 1934. The room was already crowded, but I knew my mother was very happy to have another boy, because her other boy was more than eight years older. I thank the Lord that my parents trusted God and did not do as so many did, choose abortion. You see, I would have missed a lot, and the world would not have been the same without me. I mean this literally, because you and I make a difference in this world, and each one of us is special in the Lord's sight. God says: "I have called you, you are mine." He has loved us with an everlasting love. I have felt His love and His presence throughout my journey here on earth. His presence has always been with me, and I have never felt alone. In my life, there have been many events in which the Lord graciously sustained me. In some cases, I used bad judgment, but I never felt rejected.

My parents loved the Lord dearly, and we were raised in the nurture and admonition of the Lord. Prayers and devotions were held daily in our home, and we attended worship services regularly. Music was foremost in the mind of my mother, and there was a song in the air always. Everyone in the family played an instrument or even two, with the exception of my father, who I thought, even as a seven year old, was not very musical. You see, in our church, the men and women were separated; men sat on the right side of the pew and the women sat on the left. Of course, that meant I had to sit next to my dad. His singing was off key most of the time. All the girls, five of them, played string instruments. My big brother Herbert played the harmonica and a horn. I learned to play the piano and the trumpet. In this setting, you can imagine there was always a song in the air. My mother saw to it that not one day was ever without music either by singing or playing an instrument. Her father and brother were organists, and her grandfather, brother, and his son were organ builders and organists, so it was a pretty musical family.

Around Christmas time, I can remember we also had a whole group of recorders playing and as everyone knows, Christmas songs ring in the festivities. It was a wonderful time; there was joy and excitement for all.

Christmastime was also a time of preparation. We did not go to the department stores to buy (there was not much to be had). We made mostly everything that we gave to each other. I made things out of wood with a small hand skill saw.

Things changed a lot toward the end of the war. Our mother had her first stroke in 1943 at the age of 41. That limited her ability to strike the lute any longer. Many things became hard to get, but the family made do with what was available. The hardest time was during the end of the war. The air sirens never stopped ringing day or night. One cannot imagine what that must have been like for people living in large cities. I watched with my mother from our garden as one armada of bombers after another flew over our area to bombard the city of Dresden. Dresden, which was only 60 kilometers from our town, was bombarded for 48 hours straight. It left the horizon toward this city red hot for several days. It was very scary. The city itself had a population of 500,000; in addition, it had 500,000 refugees from the East and many from Hungary. People fled to Dresden because they felt safe there. The world news report told us that the casualty count was about 136,000, but with this large number of refugees – 500,000 – the casualty count must have been much higher. Nobody knows; all we know is that the city was a incinerator with no bones or bodies to count. It was horrible to watch such an attack. As a child, I asked myself what happened to all the boys and girls my age. My mother and I prayed that the Lord would protect and save them.

We felt that the end of the war was only weeks, maybe days away; it became very dangerous in and around our town, Hartenstein. Hartenstein is located at the foothills of the Ore Mountains (Erzgebirge). Its population at the time of this story was 3,500. Hartenstein was and is a tourist attraction with many sightseeing spots, several dating back to the 11th century. The centers of attraction are two beautiful castles dating back to the 11th century as well as other buildings preserved in their original condition of fachwerk (fancywork) architecture. Unfortunately, one of the castles, the largest one, was hit by American fighter bombers, and the most beautiful part was destroyed by fire. Hitler's Schutzstaffel (SS) was to be blamed. They used the castle as a fortified center. When it went up in flames, my little sister, Magdalena, who was 8 years old at that time, could not stop crying. It was sad.

We were told by some source to raise the white flag, a sign of surrender. One time my dad was not fast enough, and we got hit in the same way as the castle. – If you do not show the white flag of surrender, you are not with us. – The damage to our house was minor; it could have been worse.

Two other incidents of American field artillery shelling were quite severe. They came in from the west, and it was the third day of the fighting; shells flew everywhere. My dad and I wanted to sleep in the bed on the first floor that night, while the rest of the family slept in the well-constructed bomb shelter. The shells hit around us very hard, and one or more of the shells hit the town's one and only movie house. When that happened, my dad and I fell out of the bed, and we hurried to join the rest of our family in the bomb shelter. The movie house was only 400 yards away from our house; it was completely destroyed.

Another interesting part of this attack was that the coal delivery company took a direct hit that night also. This company delivered the coal in wagons drawn by Belgian horses. All the horses were killed, and, since they were freshly killed, the owner sent out a message that people could come and cut themselves horsemeat for human consumption. I went there also with a knife and a pouch since my father could not go. But the people swarmed over those horses like a swarm of bees. I did not get any of the meat myself; I was too small to even get close to it.

As time went on, the American forces moved even closer to our town. I guess at that time the artillery barrages against our town were directed from a distance of 3 kilometers, from a village named Zocken. These were sporadic attacks, calculated not to destroy the German population.

The remaining German army units still were under the illusion that they were winning the war. This manifested itself in the small defense perimeter they set up on the hill not far from us, roughly 300 yards from our house. There, they established three machine gun nests embedded in three old stone quarries. Fantasizing about holding up the line against the oncoming American army, all these German fighting units were small. It was really only 15 miles to the Czechoslovakian border, and the fighting would soon be over.

My neighbor's son, Klaus, a friend of mine, and I were playing on the hillside with our scooter near our house, and we decided to visit these stone quarries. We went to the one closest to us, and we listened and observed what the German soldiers were talking about. It still echoes in my ears what they said about defeating the enemy. After spending about 7 or 8 minutes there, the Lord pulled us away in a hurry. It was then that four fighter planes appeared in the sky wiping out everything that moved. In no time, everything was destroyed at the site of the three machine gun nests. I was later told by some other neighbors who could watch this fight (engagement) from their houses that all the soldiers were killed, gone. If the Lord had not intervened and pulled Klaus and me away quickly, we would have met the same fate as these soldiers.

There were two other close encounters where I was not alone and felt the presence of angels watching over me. Although I knew the 23rd Psalm then, now, I can definitely say, "Even though I walk through the valley of the shadow of death, I will fear no evil for you are with me." As a 11-year-old kid, I had no fear. To me, these episodes were fascinating, but nevertheless very dangerous. Yet, the war was practically over, and we did not know how many German units were still in the area.

On another hillside east of our town was an artillery battery. It was hard to tell what area they bombarded. They were aiming their guns at us, but I don't believe we got shelled by them.

This is how it was during the 4 to 6 days of fighting. The American army fired their barrages, then they stopped. They came in to the upper part of the town and then they pulled out again. I didn't feel like sitting in the bomb shelter all the time. We could not go on long stretches around the city, but, within the neighborhood, one could take a peek at the fighting situation outside. That was the time when I observed another German unit moving close to our house. They were coming down the hill, on our fence line, to position themselves for a fight with a light American armored column coming down our main thoroughfare from the north of our city. I was in our garden on our side of the fence. The American army spotted that German detail, and I could tell how the turrets of their guns turned in our direction. Again, there was nothing left of that unit, and our stockade fence had also sustained a pretty good hit. Several concrete posts were chopped into pieces. I hit the ground behind an embankment and was spared from the bullets flying overhead. All these encounters I mention were obviously a lesson to teach me later in life how the Lord protects and keeps us. Psalm 139 proclaims His marvelous love. In verse 5 it tells us how his presence surrounds us from all sides and his steadfast hand shields us from above. It says such knowledge is too wonderful for me, too high for me to attain.

On another occasion, I slipped over to my uncle's house. I hadn't seen my cousins for several days, which was unusual. They had 7 boys in the family and 3 of them were about my age. In normal situations, most of my free time was spent there. This day, however, was different from any other. While we were running around, the artillery shells were falling right in front of us in an open field, and the shrapnel fell very close to us. That went on for quite some time, but we ran for safety into my uncle's house. None of the eight duplex houses in that row of the settlement were hit. The older folks could not understand what the purpose was, because the shelling went on for a long time. If the gunners had pulled back their trajectories 200 feet, that would have been the end of the houses and us.

After 5 to 6 days of war activities, the guns, large and small, were relatively silent around our area, and one could see more American troops moving into Hartenstein, to the center of the city. The commanders must have been pretty confident that most of the German army resistance was extinguished. They positioned Sherman tanks and armored personnel carriers throughout the city. One of these armed outposts was again close to our house, and it was of special interest to me. My friend Klaus, my cousin Eberhard, and I went to this spot frequently to befriend ourselves to the soldiers of a tank battalion. At that outpost were stationed two Sherman tanks, one ¾-ton truck, and a jeep. Eberhard, my cousin, and I (aged 11 years) were interested in one of the tanks, and the crew of that tank seemed to like us. They let us climb on top and inside. Our visits went on every morning; we could not get enough of it. We took advantage as long as it lasted. At that time, I owned two chickens that promised to give me three eggs in two days. These eggs were a great contribution to our nourishment in these trying days, but these eggs had to perform another function when we visited the tanks. The soldiers of that tank crew were the direct recipients of my three eggs in two days from my two chickens. Fresh eggs in the morning for these guys? One could not come up with anything better. My father was always talking about fresh eggs, ham, and bacon that he had had when he was in the United States for five years. The soldiers, in turn, gave me chocolate, candies, cookies, peanuts, peanut butter, and whatever else they could spare. We had a real good time, and my chickens were told not to stop laying.

All of a sudden, another tank column moved up on the other side of the main thoroughfare of our city. It was in the area of the so-called Fischerberg near the cemetery. We could observe this battle very clearly from our house. I counted six Sherman tanks. It was quite a sight to watch. They must have known that another German unit positioned themselves in this heavily wooded area. A terrific fire fight erupted that was actually fun to watch, not considering human lives and property being lost.

Another day went by and nothing really happened – no guns firing, no sirens, and, most likely, no casualties. But the American army was still moving east. One spearheaded to the next village called Raum, and the other moved east to the city of Aue. We could see how the army and the tanks moved, first on the main road and then over an open field. The village was occupied by Hitler's elite troops, the SS. This I am sure the Americans knew. It was just a matter of time, and the SS was eliminated. The village sustained heavy damage, but the population had moved out before the attack, so no civilian casualties occurred. I had friends in the village and that concerned me greatly. This stronghold in Raum must have been the last one the American forces conquered during this campaign around our town, an area of about ten square miles. Now, we were waiting for the total collapse of the German Reich.

And then it happened. On May 9, 1945, the total unconditional capitulation of Hitler's Reich was broadcast all over the world. Everyone, yes everyone who loved peace, took a deep breath and thanked God for his love and mercifulness of protecting us through an awful, terrible ordeal. Those who knew God and His Son our Savior Jesus gathered in churches and meeting halls to thank him for all He had done.

But still some others waited in anticipation for their loved ones – would they still be alive and come home? Like my brother Herbert who was missing in action on the Russian front and spent five horrible years in a Siberian prison camp, or those soldiers whom I had seen being killed and then dumped in a mass grave at our cemetery. How long did it take their loved ones to find out if they were still alive? It was not until Germany was united in 1989 after the wall fell. That is more than 44 years.

A very impressive scene was when thousands upon thousands of troops from different nationalities marched through our town going home, going west. They came from prison camps the Germans controlled – that massive force came from an area we did not know and never found out. But it was awesome to watch: the

French army with their flags and their music, the British army and other nations the same. It was amazing. Last came the defeated remainder of the German army. For those troops, General Dwight Eisenhower's order awaited them to be turned over to the Russians. That ordeal was the worst these guys could hope for. And some of them tried to get away before they reached where those checkpoints were. They did not know where those checkpoints were, but we knew, and we helped them not to fall into that trap ending up in the hands of the Soviets.

Chapter 2
The Time after the War

After going through a terrible, scary time during the last days of the war, needless to say, we looked forward to a period of relief, quiet, and peaceful times. As I have said, the American forces liberated us from the Nazi terror, and we considered the weeks of their occupation a real peace. However, everyone in my town and other nearby villages I know of were afraid of what was to come. We understood that the Yalta agreement between the allies would put us into an entirely different situation. We still had hoped that the lines drawn then would fall somewhat in our favor. Most of us prayed that the Soviets would not be the end result. We all knew that meant misery again.

Can you believe that I was barely 11 and understood the whole situation and so did others of my age. The Lord had other things in mind for us. As the Americans moved out, the Soviets moved in. I was literally on hand when the occupying force for our town arrived. It was a force so strikingly different from that of the Americans, those with power and might who were in full control of the last few weeks of the war, not to mention the ease with which they approached to wipe out the remaining force of the German resistance. They were in no hurry actually to finish the war, it seemed like they just played cat and mouse. So, here came the Soviets, but not with tanks and heavy guns. They arrived in the town square in two American-made 1 ½-ton trucks and a ¾-ton truck. The commander, an officer (I don't know what rank), and eighteen soldiers. Their uniforms were badly beaten from the war, rags were wrapped around their legs from below the knee to the boot, and they carried with them, of course, grease guns that did not jam up like the precisely made German rifles and pistols did. They settled into the big town hall at the town square. A day later, an order was given by the commandant that everyone who owned a German uniform, army, Schutzstaffel (SS), Sturmabteilung (SA), or any other, had to turn it into the town hall. The guns that the Germans had had already been seized by the American forces; these included hunting rifles and the like. We, as kids, always looked for what might happen next, and we were right there the next day when the Soviets put on the SS and SA uniforms with their shining boots.

During the first days of their occupation, their main objective was to clear out any resistance that would interfere with their occupation. They went through all the houses to inspect and search if anything was suspicious. My father outsmarted them. He said to us, "I won't let them search through the house and turn over everything." He had a very large atlas with the center folding pages. He put the atlas on the large table we had in the kitchen, and, when the inspection search team arrived, he greeted them and led them to the kitchen table with the large atlas sitting on the table. To his astonishment it worked. They had never seen a map before. They were so interested to find their home area from which they had come, that time went by so quickly that they had to move on to the next house. Our house was spared from search-and-destroy parties at least for three more times following the first visit by the inspection team. They could have torn out a piece of the atlas, leaving nothing left of the whole, but they didn't.

As time went on, more troops were brought in and stationed around the town. Their headquarters were moved to a former Masonic lodge.

Many stories could be told that originated during the first weeks of their occupation. Two of them are worth mentioning: My friend from class was driving down a straight stretch on his old rusty bike with his hands off the steering bar. A Russian soldier came from the opposite side with an almost new bike. He saw my friend not holding on to the handle bars. The story has it that the Russian soldier stopped him, and they exchanged bikes. My friend took his new bike and took off, looking back only to see the soldier on the ground.

In the other episode, soldiers had never seen a flushing toilet. At that time, the water reservoir was four feet above the toilet. The Russians thought that was a good place to wash potatoes, but pulling the water from the reservoir was not such a good idea as they found out. All potatoes disappeared.

Many other such stories could be told that were comical in nature; others were not and could be described as sad and vicious, as when it came to the rape of women and young girls by soldiers. Much later in life, I went to Pennsylvania to a town named Boiling Springs, a beautiful town with many freshwater springs that form lakes. On the spot, one could see many ducks and geese and other wild animals. One thing caught my attention — a female duck was being bred by 11 male ducks, standing in line to get their turn. Yes, standing in line. This episode brought to mind what some of the young girls went through in the first few months of the Russian occupation. Some of the girls were very young and, as a result of their mistreatment, could no longer function in life. I happened to know some of those who ended up with severe scars on their bodies. This all took place after the fighting stopped. I cannot imagine how the Russian soldiers treated the women in the fighting zone.

In Hartenstein, the occupation force took over the town hall and several other buildings in the square. Most of the houses in the prominent section of the town had to be evacuated; the soldiers then occupied those houses, and they became off limits to the German population.

Hartenstein was somewhat of an industrial city; there were textile factories and machine shops. After a while, the factories had to stop working, because the Russian soldiers dismantled all the sewing machines and the like. When the machines were taken apart, they were loaded on trucks and wagons to be transported to the railroad station, packed into large containers, and shipped off to Russia. These sewing machines, for instance, were not carried from the second or third floor by men in elevators or by steps; no – they were thrown out of the windows onto the trucks. There were really not many usable parts left on these machines after that. One could see long trains filled with crates hauling off most of the German industry.

From time to time, the garrison with its commandant was changed, and we hoped that the situation as far as food supply would change for the better. I don't know how it worked, but it was said that the commandant was in charge of providing food for the population in his region. Unfortunately, they did not care if we had anything to eat. There were German caretakers in place that negotiated with the commandant about everyday life situations, mostly food, but nothing seemed to work, and, as a result, starvation set in. People were dying left and right, young men and women in their thirties and forties. The rations, food that was later supplied to us to last a week, lasted only one day. What we got couldn't be stretched any further. My mother gave us her part, and she lost all her strength. She went to be with the Lord at age 44 soon thereafter.

We tried to get hold of anything that was edible, such as green apples or green pears. We had some fruit trees and berry bushes in our garden. The fruit never made it to maturity. This was bad, because the ripened fruit would have been real nourishment later on. We did not steal anything from the ones who had a little more, such as the farmers in the three nearby villages, but we went and begged them for potatoes or a piece of bread. We were very hungry. This went on for weeks, months, and years.

There are three episodes that will demonstrate how severe this starvation period really was. All this happened right around us, but there were many stories from other locations that are too numerous to record.

My father was an invalid from the First World War because of a very large injury he sustained on his fore head, the result of a shrapnel wound. Because of that injury, he became epileptic and had attacks periodically. During normal times, however, these attacks were light, did not happen very often, and were almost unnoticeable. During the starvation time, these attacks happened more frequently. On one occasion, we thought we would lose him. He was lying on the floor in our kitchen, and, for a long time, his body was shaking and jumping one to two feet in the air. It was a horrible sight for us children to watch, but we wanted to stay with him. After one of our neighbors brought some food, my father regained strength and the attack stopped.

Another neighbor happened to know that there was a freight train stopped at the station in Hartenstein, and one of the wagons held molasses. He helped himself to that molasses from an outside faucet, but that molasses did him in. It ruined his digestive system. He could not be helped anymore.

I went into my grandfather's garden and helped myself to green fruits from his fruit trees. This did not help me. I laid on the ground with my legs in the air, and all the acidity came out of my mouth as a brown-blackish syrup. There were incidents after incidents like this. This was the darkest period in my life that I had to experience.

The farmers finally got to know us, and we didn't get anything from them any longer. There was literally a whole army of beggars marching out to these farmers, and one can imagine that their supplies ran thin, but the farmer boys liked one thing I possessed very much. I had a large collection of about 3,000 stamps, and the stamps were a very good commodity to trade. These stamps helped us out with food for months. I traded for wheat, rye, barley, potatoes, and bread, in some cases. My oldest sister Elisabeth would say, "Paul saved us from starving completely." Other small gifts came our way that helped us in critical moments such as CARE packages from the Christians from the West or the USA.

One time, going to confirmation classes in the afternoon, my two sisters, two cousins, and I walked by a farmhouse. It was also a mill, and they still milled flour and grits. It was then that we saw a cat running with a brown bag in her mouth. We switched gears right away because we were sure what the cat carried in her bag were good sandwiches. We caught up with the cat. She dropped the bag, and we found four sandwiches unharmed in it. Not a full meal, but a meal we hadn't seen for a while. The bread was covered with bacon grease. We came together, broke the bread, and thanked the Lord. – Many times I was forced to eat in the same place where cows and sheep grazed in the pasture. There are several edible delicious grasses, but not total nourishment, helpful only for a short time.

As kids, my younger sister and I had to take care of the firewood supply, so we had to go very deep into the woods, digging out tree stumps and the like. A few cousins had to do the same job for their family. Although we did not always go together, on one occasion, my cousin Eberhard and I did. Although we were always hungry to begin with, on that day, we were extremely hungry. We fell on our knees and asked the Lord to give us some food. Not long after our prayer, we noticed something in the trees. It was an extra large pigeon. Not a dove, not a damsel, not any other bird that lives deep in the wood. Now, the closest farm with pigeons was at least four miles away. We knew the woods and all the surrounding area. It did not take long to realize our good Lord answered our prayer. We thanked him for his heavenly gift. Eberhard and I took up stones and hit the bird with a couple shots, and it came falling down. The bird was not sick, as we could tell, and we rushed home with our heavenly gift thanking our Lord. Eberhard's mom prepared the bird for us so all could join in such a heavenly manna. All in Eberhard's family, who were present at that time, were fed, even though the bites were small. We knew that our good Lord takes care of us, even when he says "Ask and it shall be given to you." — And remember, the Lord fed 4,000 and 5,000 men, not counting the women and children, with a few loaves of bread and some fish. If you had faith, He would do it for you also.

Under the Communist government, the food shortage, not getting enough food to nourish our bodies and consequently starving, was the number one problem. But, in our case, the monetary problem was similar in nature, because the government did not supply enough compensation so that we could live reasonably. Our father, because he could not work owing to his war injury, had to depend entirely on the compensation he received from the government. Before 1945, this compensation was sufficient for survival, actually very comfortable, but this changed after the Communists took over in East Germany. To them, all veterans were war criminals, and they should receive nothing. That was a predicament for us; needless to say, there was no money available for any special functions. For me, that meant that I had to bring in some money. The high school that I attended did not charge tuition, but other commodities did amount to quite a bit – the railroad, the books, the labs, to mention a few. I also took piano lessons, and for those I could not ask my father to pay. I made some money in an unusual way. I would collect wild mushrooms and sold them to a wonderful clientele. Or, I sold bags of sawdust from the lumber mills which served as a heating component in the wintertime. Our forests around Hartenstein were huge. I learned that we had the largest beech forest in Germany. It was very interesting to learn about all our forests, and that gave me a real peace and an incentive to study it later on, but this was also denied to me. Only the upper elite received such a privilege. I am a survivor and overcame many hurdles, and, again, I did not walk that path alone.

Considering that we were always hungry and were not taken care of by those in authority, it did not take long to dislike the people in charge and that included the Russians. Trucks with uranium fuel were passing through our town continuously. We as kids tried to disrupt some of their operations. We bombarded these trucks with stones, and the truck drivers, being Russians, would have accidents. In some cases, the trucks crashed.

It was common knowledge that the food we were supposed to be getting for our consumption, produced at our farms, was shipped out in large quantities to Russia, as it was with the machinery dismantled from our factories. It was also common knowledge, that when people are hungry over a long period of time, they get desperate quickly; hunger hurts. People revolted and uprisings were reported in many parts of East Germany. First, small in nature, as time went on, wider in scope. The people who participated in the uprisings were quickly crushed and severely punished, and punishments were handed out on their families as well. Some came home in nailed-down coffins with guards provided to suppress the true evidence of their death until they were buried. We experienced this as well, when some of our friends came home that way. This injustice by the East German government took place daily. Nothing was reported by the Western press until the last uprising in 1989 when the Berlin Wall came down. Up to this point, much blood had been shed. I and many of my contemporaries, who were 2 to 3 years too young, could not stand to witness such terrible injustices by this terrible unlawful Communist government much longer. But, we were afraid of opening our mouths; everything was recorded and transmitted to a higher authority.

Chapter 3
A Prologue to a Daring Escape

For me, I had to make a decision to fight it like others did, or to get away from it all. I could not take it any longer. In 1949, I started my plans to escape to West Germany. Before that, however, I had to finish some more schooling. Furthermore, I would have been too young for my father to consent to such an endeavor, so that is why the reason for my escape began with the harassment that I endured in the following years, in reality, the last two school years.

Surviving a horrible, destructive war, a tyranny not seen since Nero's time, carried out on people by torture and the like; mostly Christians, the German people in the East (what was called the area behind the iron curtain) had no idea what awaited them in the future. From 1945 on, as Hitler's Reich collapsed, until 1949, four regime changes took place. First came the American liberating force; their stay was short, but their presence was felt vividly in those few weeks. To me, and I know to many others, peace was almost at hand. Then, the Americans were replaced by the Russian occupational force having a somewhat German caretaker government. Then, in 1948, elections were held, under the supervision of the Soviets. Several parties emerged, but the one that received the majority was shoved over a cliff. That party was the CDU, or Christian Democratic Union. The party that did not win the election, but that announced they had won, was the East German Communist Party called SED (Socialist Unity Party). They had the backing of the Soviets and, of course, the Komitet Gosudarstvennoi Bezopanosti (the KGP). The part of Germany governed by the SED was called the DDR or German Democratic Republic. This government had no use for those who did not fall in line with their ideological thinking. Christians, therefore, were on their black list. Unless you belonged to this government elite, the situation for most people went from bad to worse. Dictatorship brought tyranny all over again; nothing had been learned from the Hitlerites.

The freedom hoped for by most people was shattered; food was still in short supply, rations were still handed out after five years, and many people died of starvation.

Chapter 4
The Daring Escape of a 16-Year-Old Boy

Now, the time for me to make a decision was at hand. Considering the political and economic situation, it was not hard for me to decide. The political pressure was too hard for me to bear. Also, I had to cut short the cycle of education in which several other privileged students and I were chosen out of my class in middle school to go to high school for four years. We had to travel 16 kilometers by train. The train picked up passengers every 3 to 4 kilometers, so that it took more than an hour to reach our destination. The city where the high school was located was Zwickau. We went to the same High School as the composer Robert Schumann did in his day: still the same rooms, same doors, same windows, and same toilets. Beside my math major, I was required to have a musical talent. All our teachers had doctor's degrees and the school was considered a small step below a University. The school day was hard and long. I had to get up at 5 a.m. and returned home at 4 p.m. In addition to the long train ride, we walked more than 1 kilometer to and from the train stations, both ways from home and at the school.

A day like that is especially hard when you do not have any food in your stomach. The school gave out a large roll to every student for lunch each day, and I was chosen for the detail to distribute that food. Many times, I was short one or two rolls and was left without getting any for myself. But the girls in the class had pity on me and shared theirs with me.

As I mentioned earlier, students who received a higher education were privileged in the eyes of the state, not that their achievement fell in the upper 10%, but that the communists saw it through a different kind of prism. My upbringing was Christian, and I did not want to have anything to do with the Communist Party (in these school years that was the FDJ or Free Democratic Youth). That was a thorn in their eyes, and so I was bombarded daily with communist propaganda. Into my second year, I'd had enough of it and told my father that I could not take it any longer. My plan was to flee to West Germany, and my father gave me his blessing. My mother would have never let me go. She would have chained me to a cement block. After all, I was a little 16-year-old kid who weighed 72 pounds.

The time came to plan for that escape. How would I do it, and where would I go? We lived close to the Czechoslovakian border, but that meant crossing two communist-controlled areas to get to the West. The other escape route from Berlin wasn't known to us, only the long border between East and West Germany running north to south. Nobody could know of my intention, except my father and a very good friend of mine, who later became my brother-in-law. How would I get to the West?

To escape to the West was on my mind long before my second year in high school. For that endeavor I needed some means of transportation, and that was a bicycle. The problem was I had none and you could not buy one. None were available. My friend, Hans Joachim, and I built one from scrap going frequently to scrap yards and junk piles where people brought their trash. He was also a fantastic organizer and had a supply of parts on hand. Hans Joachim was a good friend to have on your side. After a while, things were in place and the thing we constructed out of many different parts really looked like a bike. The time it took us to construct this bike was roughly three-quarters of a year. The only thing that was missing were the tubes and the tires, and you could not get them anywhere either.

My mother's cousin, Aunt Lilly's husband, worked in a coal mine and, from time to time, those people got an extra bonus from the government that was something in the form of items such as bike tires. I approached her and, since I knew she loved coffee with a passion, I offered her a ¼ pound as a trade. She agreed and worked on her husband, Carl, or so she said. Coffee was another commodity item one could never think of getting, but my older sister who lived at that time in the United States would send me some in a care package. The trouble was that Tante Lilly had drunk the coffee long ago, and I would never see my promised tubes and tires. I approached another miner who worked in the Uranium mine with other items of trade like peanut butter and chocolate, and I finally had the bike together. Shortly after that, I noticed a ¼ pound of coffee had a street value of 300 East German marks (roughly $75).

Now I had to figure out where I would escape along the North-South border. Several years previously we had a vicar in our Lutheran congregation in Hartenstein. This man, now a pastor, took on a call to Saalfeld, a city very close to the border about 120 kilometers west of my home. He would be one of the persons I could trust because we were very good friends. When talking with my father as his point of contact, he agreed that he was the perfect person to approach.

It was a friendly, sunny Tuesday morning, June 28, 1950, when I started out on my bike journey. As was always the case, my dad and I and the rest of the family started with our devotion and a special prayer for me for the Lord's protection on my journey. Nobody would stop me from taking a trip as a vacation, because many people did it. I estimated it would probably take me two days to reach my destination, Saalfeld. I had a blanket, a poncho, some extra clothes, and some food and drink with me. It was not much food; I remember that. The journey took me over rough terrain, mountains and valleys, I had to walk many mountain stretches, because the bike had only one speed, not a multispeed as we are used to today. Where I slept at nights, I do not remember any more. One barn and an overpass of a bridge come to my mind. The Lord was good to me. He protected me and held his loving hand over me. As a matter of fact, He was riding with me. I was a little scared, but I never felt alone. Our Pastor in confirmation class had us memorize a Christian song every week, and I could remember many of these songs. I sang them on the bike and prayed them before I laid myself down. One of those beautiful songs was: *Praise to the Lord, the Almighty the King of Creation.* This hymn would be one of the guides throughout my journey and after. The countryside was beautiful with the blooming of many trees and bushes.

When I reached Saalfeld, the pastor and his family welcomed me with open arms. They tried to persuade me not to continue on this dangerous journey, but they also understood and were very helpful. The pastor knew more than anybody what was going on at that border, because he received a daily casualty report. He told me that there was no chance whatsoever to get across the large border area he was familiar with. But somehow, where his Aunt Hulda lived, there might still be a possibility.

I stayed at the pastor's parsonage for several days and did some site-seeing around Saalfeld with my sister Sigrid. She was at that time keeping house for the pastor's family. Saalfeld and its surroundings is a most tranquil place. Beautiful mountains covered by trees of a variety of species, the valleys loaded with flowering blooms. I can remember driving through that magnificent landscape with my sister. Even riding the bike, she loved to sing and had a song in her heart most of the time. It was great with my sister and the pastor's family, but the time came to part from them. Again, no day went by without lifting up our eyes to the Lord from whom we receive everything. The pastor prayed for continued blessings on my trip and especially for my protection.

The place where Aunt Hulda lived was 180 kilometers north of Saalfeld. The terrain on that stretch was mostly flat except for about 40 kilometers out of Saalfeld. I could make better time and reached Aunt Hulda in three days.

On this part of the journey, one could see nothing but huge wheat and rye fields and that made me wonder why at home we did not have enough bread to eat. Yes, as I explained earlier, most of our production was shipped out to Russia. The road I was traveling on was strikingly close to the border itself. It ran parallel to the border, and often there were patrols of troops passing me in either direction. I remember on that stretch I slept in a rye field one night.

Upon arriving at Aunt Hulda's place, I was relieved that I had finished my tour. It seemed so tranquil there. Yet, the most dangerous task was still to come. Aunt Hulda had a small farm: two cows, chickens, geese, and other animals. This sort of lifestyle was right up my alley. I loved the farm and all that went with it. She fed me well with potatoes, butter, eggs, bacon, meats, and other goodies. I had not seen anything like it for years. She also knew already that I was coming but she had no telephone. That puzzled me. After four days doing some chores for her, things started to become somewhat risky. People started to ask who I was and where I was from and what I was doing there: all kinds of questions and you could not tell whether there was a communist sympathizer there. After talking it over with her, Aunt Hulda realized that I was going to get into trouble, and we agreed that I would leave the next morning. Yet, she offered for me to stay and I could have the farm and all that came with it. From what I could tell, besides the pastor's family, she had no other relatives. Aunt Hulda was a wonderful person, very kind and generous. She also was God fearing; she loved Jesus and His Word. I could tell that I would have had a wonderful time with her. She really needed someone to help her manage her place, but I had a goal to fulfill and that was foremost on my mind.

Early in the morning, I ate a good breakfast and took only my knapsack with me. Aunt Hulda prepared several sandwiches loaded with bacon fat for me to eat on the way. I left my bike at Aunt Hulda's, since I could not use it over the rough terrain, fields, and woods. The border was about 6 kilometers away from Aunt Hulda's house, and on that walk I had to avoid contact with anyone. I finally reached the death strip, where one could not miss seeing the movements of vehicles and guards. I sought and located an area where I might be able to sneak past. It worked for a while, but pretty soon someone called and said "Get up boy, what are you doing here?"

They knew what my intention was and took me in a vehicle to the next house, which was the border headquarters. There were Russians and East German guards by the dugouts. The Russians were friendlier than the East Germans, so I had my conversations with them, showed them pictures I had taken with me and told them of my intention to leave for West Germany. I told them that my sister, who went to West Germany early in 1947 was living there (she left when it was considered still an open border). I told them that she was hit by lightning and was lying in the hospital for over a year already and she needed someone from her family there. But they did not buy it, and they took me and shoved me up into the attic.

It was somewhat scary in the attic because nobody else was up there. After a couple of hours, at around 10:30, they took me back down and I was marched off with a column of men and women into the town of Ellrich. In Ellrich was a border prison with one side for men and the other side for women. The East German guards shoved us into the large holding cell. There were about 25 to 30 men in it. Everyone had to wait 48 hours before we would get anything to eat or drink. But around 4 o'clock the same day they pulled me out of the prison. I had to see the border magistrate or judge and explain to him why I was trying to escape. They pulled me out early because I was a minor and, to them, I looked in appearance like a little boy, because I weighed only 72 pounds. Before I got out of the prison I gave my sandwiches Aunt

Hulda made for me to those hungry guys, who to me were not criminals, and they appreciated it greatly.

In the holding cells, those who lived close by told horrible stories of what had happened in the weeks before. One of these stories was that two local men were cutting grass in the field close to the border and the border guards, coming from all different areas of East Germany, did not know if they were going to escape, so they shot them to death. At the funeral procession in Ellrich, the people walked behind the casket to the cemetery. A border guard on a bicycle drove past the procession and some people in the procession recognized him as the guard who killed these two men. A bunch of men pulled out of the procession and beat the border guard to death. Other stories were told so that I wondered if I ever should try escaping again.

When I was let out of the prison and faced the magistrate or border judge, he asked me many questions. At the end, he told me that I should never try to escape again. He also told me that he was sending me home with the communist youth brigade. I told him that I did not need them because I came by bike and was going back with the bike. He warned me, however, if I should try again I would face jail time for several years and my father would have to pay a heavy fine (20,000 East German marks). That really gave me something to think about, but I was determined, and, with the help of the Lord, I would make it. The Lord had always been on my side through thick and thin.

It was getting late and the sun was about to disappear and I was thinking should I or shouldn't I. It seemed like I received somewhat of a call that said "Go, you will make it." So I did. I walked along the town's edge and looked in the direction of the West. At that time, one young man came walking down a field road. He looked like an angel to me. I asked him if he could tell me where West Germany was. He pointed out a mountain that was mostly in deciduous trees, a remarkable difference from all the other mountains that had needle pine or fir trees. I started immediately, going not in the direction of that mountain, but turning east until I reached the edge of the woods. You see, the border guards were sitting in the open and turned their binoculars in the direction the people who escaped came from. That is how I was caught the first time. After walking quite a distance, getting tired, and the day was almost gone, I pulled out of the woods to see what happened.

You have to realize I had no idea what the border looked like. I saw three ladies on a bench enjoying the evening. I approached them and asked them if this was West Germany. They did not say anything, but motioning in the direction where four border guards were sitting in the grass roughly 100 meters away from me. They saw me, probably hearing what I asked the ladies, jumped up and chased me. I, of course, wasted no time and ran in the direction of the underbrush. Because of my size they could not follow me through the brush, but I heard and felt several shots of firearms toward me. I ran and ran until I was completely exhausted. At that time I threw myself into a bush in a small ravine near a little brook, telling myself that "This is it. I give up. If they get me now, so be it."

I rested for some time, and then I looked around for anything that might be in sight and listened for any noise. The earlier encounter with the patrol was the first perimeter; now, I had to pass a second patrol directly on the border. As I looked around, I saw a large sign about 80 meters or yards away. On the sign was written in phosphorus paint "Border Do Not Cross, Penalty Severe." I was very happy to see the light at the end of the tunnel. I crawled in the direction of the sign. I avoided guard dogs and mines, and, in a few minutes, I knew I was a free person.

Again, with the Lord's help, I made it. (After the wall fell, 45 years later, my nephew and I walked the same path that I took and we noticed a large area of marsh or quicksand to the left of my path. At the time when I was crawling, it was too dark to notice the marsh.) That marshland on the left side seemed to me some protection, because nobody, not even dogs, could get through it. When I reached West Germany that night, West German border guards greeted me and sent me in the right direction so that I would not stray back into the East; the border was not straight and that could have easily happened. The West German guards asked me, "Boy, how did you make it?" What could I answer them? It was help from above that guided me through. Three years later, a third security belt was set up, which was a 10-kilometer belt, and if you had no business in the 10-kilometer belt, you were immediately arrested.

Being now a free man, I walked that night about six kilometers to the next town with a railroad station. The town's name was Walkenried. I had only a limited amount of West German marks to get to my final destination where my sister Ruth was lying in the hospital still suffering from the wounds of the lightning strike. In Walkenried I stayed overnight in the train station where I heard horror stories one after another. There, I bought a ticket to Nordheim. In Nordheim I got out of the train station and saw, for the first time, a banana in a fruit stand. With the rest of my money, I bought nearly three pounds of bananas. I sat on the roadside and ate every one of those delicious bananas.

The next thing was for me to get up to Hannover-Land, where my sister was. I tried to hitchhike, but nobody stopped. On top of that, I made a mistake hitchhiking south rather than north. Maybe that was my luck, because there was a truck stop, and many truckers stopped there for breakfast. One truck had a sign on its doors saying it was from Hamburg, 90 kilometers north of Hannover City. I walked into the restaurant and saw two men sitting in the corner on the other end. When I asked them if they were the drivers of the Hamburg truck parked outside, they said "Yes, why?" I told them where I had come from, where I was going, and that I needed a ride to Hannover City. They said "Boy, sit down" and bought me a very delicious breakfast. After I told them how I got across the border, we started out. As we approached Hannover, they took their big rig straight through the city of Hannover. My father had given me a name of a friend from his school years and confirmation class to see. He would help me the rest of my journey. The truck drivers stopped nearly at the footsteps of his home. They also gave me some more money in case I would need it.

My father's friend put me straight to bed; I slept from 2 p.m. to 6 p.m. Then he took me to the railroad station and bought me a ticket to Rothenburg, my destination. Rothenburg was where my sister Ruth was a patient in the hospital. She had been there for over a year already and was not nearly well enough to be discharged. I arrived in Rothenburg at 9 p.m. at the railroad station, took a taxi with the money the truck drivers gave me, and went straight to the hospital. Rothenburg is not a large city, roughly 50,000 in population, so it didn't take too long to get there.

Upon arriving at the hospital, I asked the information desk attendant where my sister, Ruth Tittel, would be. I told her who I was and, since everybody in the hospital knew my sister, I was surrounded by a large group of nurses and doctors in no time even as late as it was. They wanted to know my story, and I told them as much as I could. In the meantime, something to eat was prepared for me, and then the chief surgeon gave me his office as my place to sleep during the night. They really treated me like a king, made a wonderful bed for me, and tucked me in. They said it would be better for me to see my sister in the morning, because otherwise the excitement would have been too great for her.

The next morning, they took very good care of me as far as food, washing, and getting ready to see my sister was concerned. A couple of nurses went with me to my sister's floor, let me stay outside her room and told her that they had a big surprise for her. She asked "What is it?" and was very anxious to receive that surprise. As I was called into the room, there were lots more nurses and doctors present and it was a great reunion for everyone. My sister Ruth and I ended that wonderful day with lifting our voices to our heavenly father for all the marvelous things He had done for us. Giving thanks and praise with a song none other than "Praise to the Lord, the Almighty the King of Creation." From that time on, I could visit my sister daily, and it did not take her much longer to get better. The Lord blessed both of us; her with a quick recovery, me with being the agent of help. God is good; yes God is good all the time.

I then lived for several weeks on the farm where my sister worked and where she was hit by lightning. The farmer had a large family with children, a maid, a farmhand, and an aunt living in the house of four bedrooms. The farmer kept me as long as he could, but room was a problem, so I moved on to another farm to be a farmhand for several months. My sister was discharged from the hospital soon thereafter and lived with a friend in the church family.

Chapter 5
Enjoying Freedom in West Germany

Coming to West Germany was a blessing in all respects. I could eat what I wanted, even with a limited amount of cash on hand. As a farmhand, I was given all the essentials to live comfortably there.

The most valuable aspect, however, was the freedom one could enjoy. Nobody was listening into your private conversations. Nobody forced you to take on a political ideology. You never had to watch out if your opinion was different from that of the ruling party government. It was hard at first to get used to that, but then I was still too young to ever have been too deeply involved in politics in communist East Germany. That is most likely the reason I made it to where I was.

The changes of being away from home had some effect on me emotionally. Being taken care of in a loving way by my mother and later on by my loving, caring sister Elisabeth was in stark contrast to my newly acquired surroundings. I would have never chosen a lifestyle such as a farmhand, but the circumstances warranted it. There was nothing else for me, a little guy, to do; I was still small because of the effects of the starvation I had experienced. I could not enter a work force other than that of helping on a farm. I weighed not 100 pounds yet and lacked bodily strength, but, in due time, that all came about and I thanked my Lord for all he had done for me. He rescued me from the darkness of the past and brought me to green pastures. He also had better and bigger things in store for me.

I don't know how farm life with reference to a farmhand was done in other parts of Germany, but here in Lower Saxony it was fascinating. The importance of living beings was such that a farmhand (knecht), as he was called, had his place among the animals. To the owner of the ranch or farm, a cow or a horse was every bit of value as a knecht. The house where the owners lived was attached to the stables and stalls where the animals and the knecht and maid lived. My room was right next to the best horse on the premises. It was very well sealed, but not well enough that I didn't have visitors such as mice or even larger animals. I had a regular bed but the mattress was a sack filled with straw. Beside myself, there were others who used my facility. During the night, I could feel them running over my face. The rancher liked me enough that, if I would have made a fuss about it, he would probably have given me a more decent place, but I did not plan to stay for a long time, besides that lifestyle triggered in me a loneliness (in contrast to the family life in which I was loved). The wife woke me up early in the morning around 5 a.m., and there was already work for me to do. I had to go out while it was still dark and split wood for the fire. Breakfast came an hour and a half later. I remember I cried sometimes. These people were kind people and never ever was there an inclination of harming me. That is why they let me pursue other avenues. The first was to enter into an apprenticeship, and the second was to apply for an immigration visa to enter the

United States. The apprenticeship was somewhat difficult to get into, because I was three years older than most of the students entering the apprenticeship program, which was another avenue for students graduating from elementary or middle schools. During that time period, only 25% of the students went to high school. So I was blessed again because an electrical firm took a chance with me; enrolling me in a three-year program. In this program, you went one day a week to trade school, and five days a week you learned on the job. In the electrical trade, the apprenticeship lasted three years. Most of the trades used that time frame. During the time of my apprenticeship, I stayed with an elderly couple from a local Lutheran congregation and paid them room and board. I had to travel twelve kilometers each way by bicycle. It was not an easy travel, especially during the wintertime. Later on, in my second year, I had an easier time, because I bought myself a motorcycle. I also established for myself a clientele in the electrical business that grew to a point where I had to be careful that it did not interfere with the place of learning.

The time went by quickly, and I had a good relationship with the owners and the workers of that firm. During the time of learning, I went to the American Consulate in Hamburg for an immigration visa that took several years to materialize, but I was given the go ahead in 1955. Now, with my own business established, I was making out well financially, so that my friends and the folks who were my customers could not understand why I would move on to America. Well, that was me. I came with nothing on my back, and, in this short time, at age eighteen, I had established a sizable business that most likely would have grown to something pretty big. I tried to make the most of it, but I knew that, without the Lord's help, it would not have happened. Seek the Lord and he will take care of you; that was my motto everywhere I went. Also the Lutheran Church in Sottrum was a great help to me right from the beginning, and, for me, it was a joy to participate in all its activities. It was an enjoyable time.

Chapter 6
A Two-Year Hitch

Although I liked every minute of my stay in West Germany, which amounted to a total of five years, my goal was still to move on and emigrate to the United States. Reasons for that were twofold; first, I had a desire for a higher education (in 1950, it was not possible for me to achieve that in West Germany); second, my father. He was the one that could not stop talking positively about the United States, for he lived in the States from 1924 to 1929. An unfortunate accident was the reason he could not stay there. He never stopped talking about the opportunities, the beauty, and the people, and, of course, the ham and eggs for breakfast. How could I miss going there like everyone else does, to the home of the free and the brave?

When I made my intentions known to my circle of friends in Germany they thought I was crazy, because I had many irons in the fire: first, was my electrical business that I started during my apprenticeship years, and, second, a great number of friends.

To emigrate to the United States, I needed a sponsor, to be in top notch health, and to have a job lined up. At the American consulate in Hamburg, I also was told I would need to serve two years in the military. I entered the United States in July 1955, and the US Army drafted me in 1956; I was in the United States for barely eleven months and not yet a citizen. One very important part of my life was that I belonged to a spiritual family, and this family was my church. This was my priority in Germany, and when I arrived here, in the Unites States. So it did not take me long to find a wonderful Lutheran congregation with a most caring pastor who took me into his office at the Immanuel Lutheran Church in Baltimore. This wonderful man was Pastor Eldor A. Cassens who counseled me spiritually, prayed with me, gave me advice on how to conduct myself in military surroundings, as well as in a proper Christian manner.

My induction into the US Army took place at Fort Holabird, Maryland. There we took an exhausting test for nearly eight hours. From there, we were shipped off in buses to Fort Jackson, South Carolina. What a place that was! Anyone who went through the training there can tell you what the regular expression is…it was really like a hell hole. In the middle of July, at over 100 degrees Fahrenheit, we were assigned our places in the barracks, each holding 40 recruits, most likely alphabetically. Four barracks to a company of 160 men.

The training was extremely rough, the temperatures were high, and the drill sergeants were tough. I filled my canteen in the morning at 6:30 a.m. with cold water, and an hour later the water in it was nearly hot. The heat affected me so much that I was hallucinating, walking in my sleep, crawling around the floor, and then finding myself in the morning in another recruit's bunk. This night walking could have been a terrible case against me because thieves had been active in the barracks. But here again, I was protected by the One who walked with me and never let me be alone. That is not to say that He crawled with me on the floor, but He knew that I could not help it.

The infiltration course, the gas chambers, the shoulder fired rockets, just to mention a few, were all very dangerous, but I had a mighty hand protecting me all the time.

During the infiltration course we had to crawl for about 100 yards, and machine guns were fired directly above our heads. Nobody, yes nobody, liked that assignment. For me, there was another not-so-pleasant episode. Everyone in the company knew where you came from and, to some groups or individuals, a German in their midst did not mix. War had just ended not long before, and people knew of the terrible injustice that was done to some groups during that time, and, of course, that was not to be forgotten.

Some buddies warned me of one individual to watch out for, but nothing happened because he fell out owing to heat exhaustion and the length of the strenuous fifteen-mile march. Extra large guys just didn't make it. Actually, all the large guys were lying on the road side because of heat exhaustion.

Basic training for the first eight weeks came to an end, and the drill sergeant let it be known that I received the best assignment in that company. Not many elevate to the rank of sergeant in a two-year period, but my military occupational specialty (MOS) would just give that to me. My MOS called for communication specialist in a battalion. I attributed this special gift to the battalion commander (colonel) in basic training.

He learned that, no matter what, that I would always look out for my army buddies first, and that is why

I got this fabulous assignment to the Infantry School at Fort Benning Georgia, skipping another 8 weeks of basic training. What a blessing that was. The reason for my getting this assignment was the following: In this particular week, we were in the field, in tents, and I was on guard duty for our platoon. An inspection by the higher ups, the commanders, was scheduled. But, as most of us can imagine, the tents were a mess. I went to work in a hurry and straightened out most of the tents except three. That was no easy task in the hour and a half until the inspection team arrived. They were surprised that the tents in our platoon were orderly. All these guys from the other three platoons coming in that evening had to go back out for another long march, poor fellows. They also missed the treat we had in the evening. Yes, that was the only pass time that we had during the eight weeks of training; for anything else, we were too tired. A local merchant came through the camp and brought us chocolate milk, milk, cookies, cigarettes, and the like. It was a good thing for most of us, but a bad thing for some. Why? Because with a $70 a month income, one could not go on too large a shopping spree. Some did and they spent their $70 plus interest they paid to some fellow recruit lenders in a hurry. Principle and interest took all of the $70 they had. I mention this to give an account of how life in the US Army was conducted under certain circumstances. Lending and spending was almost the same as at home. Those soldiers who dealt in the money market made out quite well. The ones who took out a loan went deeper and deeper into the hole

I skipped the next eight weeks of basic training at Fort Jackson and moved on to Fort Benning, Georgia. In Fort Benning, things looked almost like civilian life. We had rooms instead of barracks, classrooms as teaching facilities, entertainments, time off, stores, movie houses, etc. One could really like it there. I liked it there a lot. One treat was that our classroom had a view of the jumping towers. And once in a while, the soldiers had their practices. It was very interesting to watch. We started out with a class of 55, but only 28 of us graduated. The class was arranged in tables of four men each. At my table, there were Tex, Tonkin, Larkin, and myself. Tonkin and Larkin came from the University of Alabama (ROTC), and Tex was from Texas University. All students in the class had a lot more education than I had. There were two sections, a theoretical and a practical section. In the theoretical section, you had to read a lot of communication material and take tests; in the practical section, you had to fix, for instance, a unit such as a 28-circuit heterodyne receiver. In the theoretical section, the other three at the table outdid me. But, in the practical areas, I probably fixed all the four units on the table. As a result, Larkin and Tonkin took me to their homes in Alabama, taught me how to play football, even though they were twice as big as I was, and took me roller skating in Phenix, Alabama. In other words, they showed me a great time. To me, if you had to be in the Army, Fort Benning was the place to be. Nevertheless, when I was given the choice of staying on as an instructor or moving on to Fort Leonardwood, Missouri, I chose Fort Leonardwood.

After a sixteen-week course in communication, I was on the way to Fort Leonardwood, Missouri. We traveled by train, and I saw some states that I had not seen before. On arriving there, I asked the First Sergeant where we were headed to. I was told that our unit, the 63rd Engineer Battalion, was assigned to Giessen, Germany. That was actually OK with me. It was known that I escaped from communist Germany. With that on the table, I was still promised a security clearance, but that all changed when we came to Germany. I was bumped out of my classical communication section and was put at the last spot in squad 4, Company B. I was very angry and did not care what I said to anyone. I could have walked out of the gate since I was still a German citizen, but I loved the United States too much.

Being in the squad for three months, I adjusted and had several breaks. One time, a bugle detail was needed for the post in Giessen, and my trumpet experience put me on that detail. The detail did not last long; our duty was two days off and one day on. One man could not stomach all the time off. He cracked up and confronted his battalion commander with an M1 rifle and was put into stockade. The rest of the three of us got put back into the squad.

Another break was that I had the privilege of accompanying the Major of the S3 section as an interpreter when he and his wife and the mayor of the town and his wife went out for dinner to discuss the building of soccer fields, forest roadways, and other projects the 63rd Engineer Battalion could construct for them. We did many such projects.

Also, every unit of the American forces had to perform border duty on the East-West German border. When it was the 63rd's turn, I and several others patrolled such a stretch with mounted machine guns on the jeep. I thought it was a bad idea to put me in such a position, because if there would have been a cry for help, I would have caused for certain an international incident.

While I was in B Company, we went on bivouac and infiltration courses. While on bivouac, several of us did some things against army regulations. We talked to guards of the camp and told them we would take a few hours off during the night, go through the woods into the village and have a good time, eating bratwurst and sauerkraut and potato salad, drink some beer, of course, and promised to bring back goodies to them, which we did. Nobody turned us in; besides, the second highest ranking noncom officer SFC Hamilton enjoyed everything we brought back. The detail that went into the village consisted again of four guys, Bihn, Rose, Tex, and I. On one occasion, we almost lost Bihn; he could not follow because it was dark in the woods and we had trouble locating him. He was from Chicago and was not used to such a rough ride. But everything turned out OK.

On one occasion, on a cold day in February 1957, we built a bridge over the Main River. It had to be done in four hours putting it up and four hours taking it down. After that was completed, we packed up wet and muddy on to the infiltration course in Wildflecken (a huge army training area). We got to an assigned area, or so they said, unloaded, and took sea rations for dinner. I had sardines and peaches and then we slipped into our sleeping bags for the night. To erect a tent was impossible. The snow was heavy, at least four feet deep. In the middle of the night a tank column rolled into our area and we were almost run over, but someone jumped up and waved them to stop on time. It was not unusual that we did not hear these tanks, we were completely wiped out. Others in the company had experienced that, so we were not alone. The Lord watched over us.

Finally, I got the break of my life in the US Army. All the work on the post in Giessen was performed by Germans, electrical, plumbing, carpenter, etc. The Army wanted to save those expenses and put soldiers with the same skills in its place. I was chosen to do the electrical detail over the whole post and was given two extra men. On one occasion, we were asked to install fluorescent lights in a huge hall housing atomic cannons. This hall was so huge we had to use the local fire department's ladders. When finished I summoned all three battalion commanders (who were colonels) to demonstrate our progress. To our astonishment they gave all of us, without hesitation, a three-day pass. And, for me, I had a three-day pass every weekend for my remaining time served in the Army in Giessen, Germany, which was close to one year. During that one year, I put that unbelievable gift of free time to real use.

The area in Germany where I lived before I emigrated to the USA was called Lower Saxony. I had a lot of friends there, and it wouldn't be out of the ordinary that I might have a friend for life there. Well it was just that. It is said, here in the USA and also in Germany, that marriages are made in heaven, but I believe that we have to help in the process a little bit as well. The time was right for me and most likely for that young lady I looked for. I had previously made several attempts, but, for one reason or the other, it did not work out. Then, there was one of my best friends whose sister I had an eye on, but she did not want any part of it. My friend suggested and introduced me to his cousin. Now, she was the one you could not miss even in a very large crowd. She almost flipped when her dad did not want any part of it. He said, "A GI? You must be kidding! Bad reputation!" He may have been against it, but all the ladies were for it. They worked for it so that it was going to be a success. So we started dating, and didn't that three-day pass come in handy. Hannover, where my bride-to-be lived was 400 kilometers away from Giessen. I did have a car which was, with a $90 month, a miracle. I forgot to mention that, while I was stationed in Giessen, I had a deal with two local car dealerships, selling cars to the newly arrived GIs in the Giessen and the Friedberg areas. That, besides selling American cigarettes on the German market, gave me that much needed cash for traveling such a distance every weekend. I could not help but to think that our (my bride-to-be and me) being together was by divine design.

Although I had some disappointments in the army, the good times outweighed the not-so-good times. In June 1958, I was honorably discharged and returned home to my beloved home in Maryland.

Chapter 7
Settling Down in the USA

My active Army time came to an end in June 1958; I served just a little less than two years. I received my honorable discharge papers at Fort Hamilton, New York. The officer who handed me these papers was a second lieutenant. One would think that during such an important epoch in a person's life, a soldier with a higher rank would do that honor, but no, kindergarteners have a much higher ceremonial departure than a contingent of troops serving this country. From there, I was assigned to a medical support unit in Baltimore, serving several more years in the US Army reserve, but, because I had enrolled in college at Johns Hopkins University, that duty was waived.

Now I embarked on a new beginning in my life, here, as a citizen of this great country the USA. When I arrived in 1955, this country gave me a lot of opportunities that anyone coming here could pursue, yet, I had to get my army time out of the way, and then the thinking and planning process was set in full gear. This second beginning was a lot different than the first beginning. I was much better equipped with my English. It was not perfect, but closer to it. But, unlike my first beginning where I met people everywhere, in buses, on street corners, in shops, all I had to do is open my mouth and there was a conversation and, in some cases, friendships in the making. (I believe this country has the friendliest people on the earth.) Was it because of my knowledge in English or the lack of it that they wanted to show me things and help me to get along? It could be said that people went out of their way so far as to share their last shirt with me. One of those episodes is really worth bringing writing about. Now, this was in 1955, about four weeks after I arrived as an immigrant. It was on a Saturday morning, when I went to the Greyhound bus station to catch a bus going to New York City to visit a relative of one of my bosses in the electrical trade business. I was somewhat reluctant to take this trip by myself, being in the states only five weeks and going into the largest city of this planet. At that time, I lived with my sister Christa and hoped to persuade her to come with me. But after several unsuccessful attempts I just had to do it by myself, and the package I had to deliver was somewhat overdue. Well, I entered the bus leaving Baltimore going to New York exclusively, therefore a pretty long stretch. It was then as I got on the bus, that a well-dressed gentleman approached me to join him in the seat next to him. While I already had a mark on a seat on the right side of the rows picked, I thanked him and took my seat directly opposite him. But he insisted, naming ladies, who may enter, being somewhat overweight, and taking more of their seat than allowed. I thanked him again, but did not join him yet. Wouldn't you know it, at that precise moment, a lady entered the bus with that description, he nodded toward me, and I accepted his invitation. The lady was very concerned about her interrupting our trip. We assured her that it was not the case; nevertheless, she got up and moved to the front of the bus. But for me, I did not move back to my original seat. This trip was such a delight, one could not imagine that such a thing existed. This man invited me to his studio in New York, for he was a music voice teacher, teaching full time at Peabody Conservatory of Music in Baltimore and part time in some studio in New York. Unfortunately I could not make it to his studio in New York at this time, but during the entire trip we had the most interesting and delightful conversations. He loved composers similar to those I liked, and Johann Sebastian Bach was number one. One cannot imagine how things developed after mentioning Bach's name.

He gave me precise directions how to get to my final destination with the New York subway; he even bought me the tokens for it. I had nothing to fear in this large city, because he gave me all I needed to know.

We parted and he gave me his standing invitation to his home in Baltimore where he and his beautiful wife awaited me to be their guest on many wonderful evenings. During one of these evenings, he had his private students here in Baltimore sing and perform their talent on musical instruments at his house. It was delightful and amazing. Sadly, after several months of a wonderful friendship, I received a call from his wife that my friend George Pollek had gone to his heavenly home.

The acquaintance with George Pollek and his wife was short-lived after I arrived in the United States, and it was like the time before I was drafted into the US Army. Two years elapsed, and after my discharge and being back home in Baltimore, I checked to see how my friend George's wife was getting along, but things seemed to be completely different than when George was still alive, so I left it as it was.

Now, I had to set things in motion and I was checking to see if I could get my job back, the one I had before the army drafted me.

I worked as an electrician at Johns Hopkins University, but Dr. Hamburger, who was in charge, told me that my job had been filled by a Hungarian refugee who had to support four children. By law, I could have demanded that I would get it back, but I waived that right considering this man's situation. Dr. Hamburger gave me hope that a professor in the electrical engineering department might need me if he received a grant from the air force. I did find other jobs in the meantime, even though there was a recession in 1958. But after several months, I received a call from Dr. William H. Huggins who interviewed me and hired me on the spot to help him build a huge analog computer. I had to quit my job with Bough Chemical Company in East Baltimore that gave me nearly double in take-home pay than I was offered at Hopkins. But the environmental and academic surroundings could not be met by any money amount.

I was blessed also to work with Dr. Huggins, a wonderful man, a genius of highest caliber. The Johns Hopkins Electrical Engineering Department hired this man after his graduation from MIT, giving him a full professorship. Huggins had a harpsichord in his office. He played it beautifully. His photography was marvelous, and one could go on and on of the quality of this individual. And here I was working with this brilliant man for more than five years. I had five wonderful years and got acquainted with all the faculty of the Electrical Engineering Department and was inducted into its ranks. Also, during this time, I got to know many other faculty members in different departments.

The analog computer was completed in two years, and, from then on, it became the basic tool to help graduate students to receive their masters or doctorate degrees in their specialties. The analog computer lab, as it was called, produced, if I am not mistaken, sixteen doctorates and two master theses. Working with these special people was another wonderful treat and a gift to me. We had an awesome relationship not just working; we also had our time of fun.

Several of the faculty members at the University, Dr. Beardon in Physics and Dr. McNicols in Biophysics encouraged me to enroll in a doctorate program, but for me receiving a BS degree from Hopkins was enough for the time being. Moreover, I had to devote my time to my wife and the little family we had just started.

After five years, the analog computer had outlived its usefulness and was replaced by the much faster digital computer, which also somewhat eliminated my position in the analog lab. Dr. Huggins wanted me to stay with him working in the digital world. At this time, however, I had no interest in it. One could say that my feelings and accomplishments in the analog world were hurt a little by being pushed out the door by the digital advancement. Maybe I should have realized that it was science advancing.

It was however very difficult for me to leave Johns Hopkins University with its great and wonderful people and a superb academic and natural environment. It happens that one of the graduate students receiving his doctor's degree in the analog lab accepted a position at the University of Maryland Medical School. He asked me to join him at Maryland, which I did, and that is where I spent thirty-two years of my life, first in the physiology department and then in the ophthalmology department. In physiology, it was all research, but in ophthalmology, it was research and patient care. I know how I ended up in these fields, but it would be too difficult to explain. I loved my work tremendously; the patient care part was exceptional. In research, I was able to publish several papers as well as a number of abstracts, which was gratifying.

My wife, Ruth, you may recall, was the one whom I met during my army time in Germany. It was then when I was able to drive to Hannover from Giesen roughly 400 kilometers each way. This was only possible, because I was given a three-day pass every weekend for the last eight months of my remaining time in the US Army. You will say, how lucky can you get. Well I think it was really by design and there was nothing I could have done for it or against it. My Lord knew what he was doing, and, as it is said, marriages are made in heaven. We are the ones who break it.

Everything from now on was done in the same manner as before. We two, Ruth and I, were never alone. We included our the Lord Jesus into the midst of our activities. Try it one time, and you will be amazed at how things in life will be going.

As time went on, we raised one child and then another and another until we had a family of six children, four boys and two girls. Again, how blessed we were, all six of them in great health, very prosperous and intelligent, staying away from drinking, smoking, drugs, and the like. You will say how can this be in the politically correct climate we are living? My wife and I trusted the Lord, and he helped us to raise our children. The yearly income I had was not great but sufficient; we struggled sometimes to make ends meet, but here again we received help from above. The first five years of our marriage, we lived in a moderate home, a duplex in the Baltimore-Hamilton area. I promised myself, however, that I would never in my life starve again. We looked for a place in the countryside and settled on a piece of land in Harford County, Maryland. It was a thirty-four mile trip to work every morning, but the area and its beauty were worth it. A moderate-size house was built on that ten-acre plot. It had a stream on it, and a fish pond was added. I raised cattle and sheep for our consumption and also for sale. As long as I live, and with the Lord's guidance, we will never starve again. I also promised myself that I will give to my children things I did not have in my childhood and that they could enjoy. I did not have a bicycle or ice skates. They could swim in the pond, also fish in it. They could skate there and sled down the hill on our property. I also let them have certain kinds of animals like a sheep, a steer or a horse, special ducks like wood ducks, mallards, and mandarin. I believe they had so much more. We all love this place; they had fun all along.

I am an advocate of higher education and wanted my children to succeed in school. Four of the six did and even went beyond the bachelor degree. Two of them received a master in electrical engineering. One daughter is a teacher, the other an occupational therapist, of their own choosing.

Now, all of our children are happily married and having their own families and we are blessed to be having a wonderful time with fifteen grandchildren.

For me, my activity in the United States has been well rounded. I was involved in PTA, cub scouts, and very heavily involved in the Lutheran Church, serving as an organist and choir director. I served on the organ bench for sixty years of my life, mostly just honorary. Even in the US Army, a Baptist chaplain asked me to play for the troops. They gave me a little pump organ to play in the field. An absolutely rewarding event was an Easter morning service in 1958 when we were in the field worshiping Jesus with more than three thousand troops – an awesome event.

I also was involved in helping to build a completely new church building. I tell you, it is very rewarding when you consider all the things you can do with your hands. I am also very successful carving with wood. You see there is for me never a dull moment in life. I do not even have enough minutes in a 24-hour day, but when I look back on my life and my walk on this earth for roughly 700,800 hours, I can only express my sincere gratitude for all the things I have been able to accomplish. In this book, I have only mentioned some highlights from my life. For me, to escape at the age of 16 from the heavily fortified, patrolled area on the East-West German Border, I can only marvel now that I made it. As the West German Border guard surprisingly expressed in his statement, "Boy, how did you make it?" But, again, my help came from the Lord who made heaven and earth; yes, I could have never made it on my own – and I know that I was never alone.

Appendix

These are pictures taken after the collapse of the communist empire. They show areas of the exact escape route, 48 years thereafter.

1. The rural landscape.
2. The area headquarters where I was kept prisoner in the attic for a short time.
3. The benches where the ladies were sitting, giving me the sign of the guards being in the immediate area.
4, 5, 6. The fence with bloodhounds running in between, also watch towers.
7. Family picture
8, 9. Bethlehem Gemeinde (post-World War II)
10. Route of escape
11. Paul Gerhard Tittel 1949
12. Paul Gerhard Tittel 2014

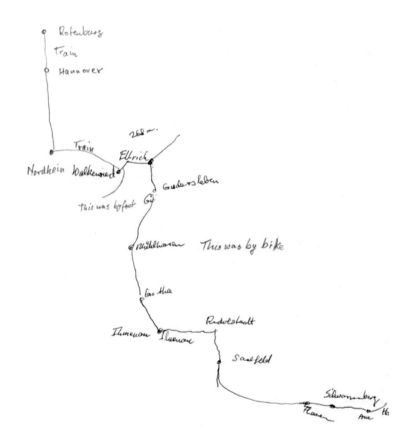

Paul - Gerhard Tittel 1949

74

Paul Gerhard Tittel - 2014